Alchemies, Arrivals

Poetry Chapbook by:

Sophia Pinto Thomas

QUILLKEEPERS PRESS

Copyright © Sophia Pinto Thomas, 2025
Book Cover Design by David R. Thomas
Illustrations by David R. Thomas
Edit by Stephanie Lamb and Margo Perez
Format by Quillkeepers Press

All rights reserved. No part of this book may be reproduced in any form or by any electronic or mechanical means, including information storage and retrieval systems, without the permission in writing from the publisher, except by a reviewer who may quote brief passages in a review.

This compilation contains some works of fiction. Locales and public names are sometimes used for atmospheric purposes. Any resemblance to actual people, living or dead, or to businesses, companies, events, institutions, or locales are completely coincidental. Any references to pop culture are owned by their specific companies and are not the property of the author.

There are some poems here within that represent the thoughts of the author. Any resemblance to actual events, locals, or persons, living or dead, is entirely coincidental.

ISBN: 979-8-218-64730-8

Published by Quillkeepers Press, LLC
PO Box 10236
Casa Grande, AZ 85130

Poems

All the Time	5
A Daughter	6
Forehead Crease	7
Alchemies	9
The Highway	10
Wits and Weeds	12
Status I	14
Bring Attention	15
for my grandchildren, in case the forests die.	16
When You Plant a Seed	18
Homeland	19
City Girl	20
City Bird	22
Chronic	23
Boston Birthday	24
Thoughts of a Shadow	25
Miserly (the Willow Project, 2023)	26
all of my faculties now…	27
The Twins	29
walking on the beach	30

Medicines	31
Lavender	33
Scalpels and Seedlings	34
The Sisters	36
Status II	37
Lilac Sky	38
valley bird	40
(A) Mother	41
for my grandchildren, when we save the forest.	42
Journey of an Herbalist	44

All the Time

I'm making choices all the time

that seem to stun, or shine.
Dripping pine and kerosene,
I'm searching for the fire...

Everywhere I go, it seems
I fall much higher, down upon
my hopes — and dreams — of yesterday.

Burning all the time.

A Daughter

A daughter is a gift —
but please don't worship her.
Power has a sound unheard,
      never unexplored,

& I don't take the maps as true!
The woods wherein I stand —
they soon reveal a wordlessness
      I know across the land —

that makes the weeds expand,
unbuckling the asphalt.
Mauves disrupt the coldest grays,
      saplings learn to stand,

but stay — with me — when I release
my ramblings of hail,
where maps don't tell me anything.
      A daughter — is a gift — of nails.

Forehead Crease

My grandmother said
to me, when
I was small:
don't let anything
touch your lovely
face. You're beautiful.
Now she's gone,
I'm grown up.
If I accent
the crease between
my dark brows,
a sharp mar
of worn beauty —
if I glare
lovingly on every
street in town,
endure their stares
at warm beauty;

if I look
with tense eyes
to indent this
line on my
forehead, will it
serve as a
small pure scar?
Will it protect
me through all
of the city?
A faint line
between my eyes
isn't the look
I'm afraid of.
The fierceness etched
in creases brings
no curse or
loss to me.

Alchemies

To soak, to dry, to crouch, to fly.
Like yarrow, I am healing
from the nothings and the cataclysms
musing in the sky.

(I read the books and studies
that have told us what we're doing.)
(libraries are armories,
pencils turn to knives.)

To pause, to run, to fight, to cry:
like arsenic, I'm screaming
to be *something* that can save a world,
or help those people — *dreaming*.

I've heard the news, and learned the songs
constructing all the present;
Now I study herbs, and words,
to show me how — *to mend*.

The Highway

The highway is split
open with every *'why'* cried out
by the trees.
The sharp guardrails cut past
the woods, but can't rival
the strength of saplings.
A river, like an otter, slips
beneath the bridge, through the marshes,
and the clouds sink rain
into the grass.

The ground is hoping —
The highway is cut open by
soft heat that tumbles from the sky.
Asphalt gasps, alarmed
at its own
impermanence — next to
the moss and stems
encroaching on the hard gray lanes.
That river rises.

Gray is challenged
by endless green,
the highway feels self-conscious.
The trees wail *'how'*
into a sky full of tears,
and the highway crumbles —
beneath them.

Wits and Weeds

At the end of my wits, I find birdsong.
Like spring, it slowly unravels — into my mind;
a screaming vengeance
of the early morning light.

Don't ever forget! — the birds alarm —
Urbanity is deep and ecological!
A richness that surpasses stone,
and bursts the yard.

The end of my wits is (ec)static,
stubbornly growing — like sidewalk weeds.
Here — away, or (re)moving
come the seeds we never see,

& the weeds reach out to an ocean
that will come to drown the asphalt.
At the end of my wits — a tree grows —
and the birds come screaming — *home*.

Status I

Walking You is moving
with the status of the ground,
where all (Y)our tensions lie —

the growth inside, like lichen, listens.

The movement soon reflects
Your place in places, self with selves.
Bodily — involves a means

to strike — or sing — the ground.

Bring Attention

Places fall and form, across
the memory of vision —
Every street or meadow path
has left me with a feeling:

like asphalt low beneath my feet,
or leaves behind my skin —
where moss has grown through both my shoes
that muse with all the water,

where cities are bemused.
My places fall and flare
against precision, I am trying
like the missionary — tides —

and all the places murmur me —
they say, *go on, keep walking
every street. And where the land is scarred,
at least you bring — attention.*

***for my grandchildren,
in case the forests die.***

here my heart harbors
fragments of fragments —

the burning glow confiscates my fear,
and turns it to moss; to bark.
mulch beams green into tiny cells,
and the stream runs into the arms of the bog,
where the water becomes a pond,

and the birds return with my heart.

the trees have thought of everything
before we forgot — or returned.
bears and deer keep time
with something
deeper than stone, broader than ferns.

where the stream curls herself
in the arms of the wetland,
the pondside holds all of the brightest birds.
They return to the ocean
of trees in my heart — the breathing
that lives in my chest wall.

When You Plant a Seed

A dull crackle. The salamander blinks,
and the soil swells — microbes look around
eyelessly for the tilling —
where did it come from?

The mycelium is elated by
perturbation. Grounds — shift, and water drinks down
through the blue peat and deep gold. The forest glances up
at soft crashings of a ripple.

The seed dives down and shivers hotly —
a flicker of dark, before
the birches raise dawn out of the woods to say
wordlessness; ground stretches, frogs are still,
until a chord is carefully formed.

The seed hears music snatched
from the sun — into the rootways
roll notes, and the soil shudders —
a tiny part planted is unaware of what it can grow,
but mycelium knows. The oak watches;
the salamander glows.

Somewhere else the leaves dip
waterfalls into embers and don't hear the springs retreat,
through the golden peat and cold cobalt.
A seed planted yesterday
has been lifted into
the somewhere of somewhere — close.

Homeland

I cast my mind on miles —
like clouds that follow over us,
I am all the acres from
the city to the shore.

(Mama has a garden.
Dad is safe at work, or home,
friends and brothers walk the street.
I've never been alone.)

I steel myself — in oceans,
and wash across the acres —
Nothing else recalls to us
the places we have known,

and flying — d(r)iving — over
seas of homes, and trees, and biting walls —
I have cast my mind across
the miles of a homeland.

City Girl

Stern jaw, squared with the buildings.

As stubborn self conscious as cheekbones
and nondescript eyes,
they're brown — and burn for no reason.
Our cities don't know how to lie.

You make up for you with intensity,
and leave all the looking defenseless
with cautious self consciousness.
You stare it in,
      with steel from the softest of flowers

that grow from the cracks in the sidewalk,
despite all the sneakers and tires —
and then, your sharp jaw softens as

you square your accounts with the street;

City Bird

I built my soaring — spires
out of scraps of tin, and rubble.
Something slashed my shoulder blades,
and wings grew out of blood —

lifting, lifted — holding, held
by scaffolds of the skyline
raising me, with all the city —
teaching me to fly.

Chronic

Chronic — [and don't be sardonic.]

        is a limitless — of loneliness.
It comes as quiet as birds — of March,
when the cold has all been welcomed.

I call to the gulls and the peregrines:
furnaces cool, the crocus reblooms!
Months of pining soon renews
        in plaintive — *please reopen.*

I'm watching the floodings, and hoping:
re/ravel a season of changes and plans,
where I stand — I stand
        on the edge of my lonely.

Chronically — [running to stand;]

Boston Birthday

I want to walk away from them,
in my burgundy birthday dress.
I want to walk away from them all,
for my entire city.

If men are our fortunes disguised,
and pigeons the kings of everything —
I'll act like the daughter I always am,
announcing my nuances then.

What am I, leaking color
in a blaze of angry belovedness?
A birthday candle, dripping wax
and thought across the road.

I walk with the city to the sea, and back,
a burning woman, wishing;
*Will the expectations emigrate
to follow me — again?*

Thoughts of a Shadow

Please my love, I pray you pay no mind
        if I am ghostly.
I look away, across again,
        my misty hands entwined.

(Come walk with me, where disconnection reigns
        and I am far from me.
Come walk across the waves that flow,
        and never make me leave.)

Come walk with me across the sun,
        where we shine by one another —
all my rainful hands, my love, are yours
        for how you will.

(Please, my love, don't pay no mind,
        if I am just a shadow.
A shadow knows the truth of things,
        and always follows through.)

Miserly (the Willow Project, 2023)

The problem with retail is miserly.
The same old woman comes in each day,
searching for our jewelry —
she's hobbling and mumbling.

She bends at the counter pensively,
searching for gemstones (what does she need?)
to fill in the gaps — of a nebulous need
with treasure — all our treasure.

Oil is coveted tirelessly
in the lands of ice and diversity.
A willow is bending our futures
down with it — snap! And then spills the arctic —

The plight of our country is miserly,
like the customer hoarding her silver.
They come in with pockets and purses of money,
all full —until we are emptied.

all of my faculties now...

It will get hotter each summer.
Food will get more expensive, I think,
people will struggle...
things may grow scarce.

Boston will flood.
The summers will get hotter,
the winters will melt,
and animals will die.

All of my faculties now — I know —
are devoted to something
more detailed and damaged than me.
With everything I may know,
give to the children —
the chances we keep...

for birds —
       and bees
       and flowers...
       trees and suns and streams.
Oh, my dear earth,
I miss when your crying
was not quite so loud —
when we were all free.

So now, it gets hotter.
Seasons — flood.
Winters — warm,
my futures all plead

with me, the novice
I am right now:
employ all the novelties,
plant every seed,

hold all the children.
Plan every ending.
Someday, the earth
and her people —are free.

The Twins

Eloquence and Anger
are the twins that bring the thunder:
lightning snaps a focus
and it shatters into rain —

Eloquence and Anger
are the siblings of Asunder,
storming through the raging clouds —
antidotes to pain —

walking on the beach

no i don't want to sleep —
i walk the beach with the rosehips
and wonder who was here before
we killed them / before
the planet was conquered by money
that mocks each home of
the soaring seabirds / so no
i don't want to sleep —

i note the small things still
growing / despite the fences
and asphalt paths / throughout
this country of lying and lied-to —
the saltwater colors the breeze
where i am hungry because
i want to be peace (and) full —
like tides in the moonlit sky
when it fades forever in pink —

where the rosehips rot by the breaks —
no i don't want to sleep / i want
to breathe where the seabirds
are never endangered —
where we can do more than eat —
surviving this land
of money and meat —

Medicines

In a forest facing Boston,
I'm trying to find the flowers
that will urge me much faster than words.
I know there are things
in missing, in waiting,
in edges that fly from me.

Rose hips and ginger are the medicine
for a body that knows what hurts.

On a highway racing Boston,
I'm looking for the oak leaves
and summer breeze that can push me:
take me in(to) the ocean
over a similar tidal plain.
I know I need to do something
before I can, before I stop.

Tea leaves and yarrow are the medicine
for a mind that is always outside.

In an ocean bracing Boston,
I'm returning to my wits, the birds, for food.
Some things will need to be written, before
I can sleep among the dunes.
The marshland (re)calls
every moment and morning
I find (in) my scattered cells.

The ocean feels like medicine
for a body that knows what's wrong.

Lavender

That summer, I was lavender
growing over the sidewalks, and
I learned the weeds and herbs to brew
to make my father sleep deeper.

I read somewhere that we must use
what seems useless, appropriate
what would annihilate us.
I learn to steal time and be smart about it,
they drain our lives, so what's
a few lost dollars? I give them instead
to the homeless man,
and pick lavender walking home.

My mother laughs at me — I'm learning
all the herbs, for homemade medicine.
She was always a skeptic, a breaker of rules
that disserve her, and now her children
are thieves. I pour the kettle
over peppermint leaves.
Ginger for the stomach,
yarrow for the bones,
sprigs of soft purple in the kitchen, so

my father sleeps a little deeper;

I learn to make use of all the things
we thought were merely weeds.

Scalpels and Seedlings

The gift arrived — with scalpels,
and needles threaded new.
All my tears dried up at once,
sympathy — removed.

All emotions came to curb
the flooded brook, renewed —
All my hands were held in scars.
All my feet kept moving —

And everything across
the ancient street spoke out to me.
Relations stopped the morning, with
the birds and children — so at peace.

And all my gifts of skillfulness
stopped before the gaps across the green.
I had no tears to cry,
I had to plant — the seedlings.

The Sisters

Endurance is the olive tree
that never bends, nor flees.

Defiance wears a glaring face
that softens to the birds.

Endurance is courageous,
but the courage comes — & then it goes;

moving forward carefully,
the pair of them — are waiting.

To witness — is to honestly
pay prayers to all persistence,

& living is resistance.
life should be for free.

Endurance in the orchard
& the desert — move relentlessly;

Defiance walks abreast of her,
& poppies start to grow.

Status II

Walking You is moving like
the whales across the sound —
slow, where every tide has turned
necessities around.

You grow among the sand dunes, and
along the surf — across the ground —
All You are comes walking
with — the status of a cloud.

Lilac Sky

i stand above the river
in a sea of lilac sky
we never know that all we need
is breaking wings to fly —

A butterfly inside a cage
will snap her wings to bend them,
and all above the opal river —
lilacs seed — the sky.

Across above, and deep below
the gold that makes a skyline:
purple of the evening
i can stand within — and cry,

until my wings may shatter out —
along the living river,
planting all the lilac seeds.
& then i finally — fly

valley bird

daughters fix their Awls upon
the marks among the stars,
and there they pierce the sky —
    or remedy a song —

silvering the birches
is a mother of her joy,
to hug so long — and kiss not once,
and never know goodbyes.

where all across the valley — cries
that bird of self protection;
she flits above the grasses
and she lives throughout — reflection —

and never drops the All
of daughterhood, and songbirds
or where they meet the sky —
to remedy — the song.

(A) Mother

I touch every child beside me.
No, I will not be a mother, except
to be one for the earth — instead.
    womanchild, waiting.

Within me, eyes of open gold —
tiny limbs, like saplings
to survive the megafire.
    and what will they derive

from all our many failures?
Everything I mother now,
with hands of opal, open eyes
    will mother them, in turn.

***for my grandchildren,
when we save the forest.***

my heartbeats thicken and steady,
into an ocean of breathing trees.

it harbors the minerals golden,
something is growing, burning my fear.
the nerves turn back into bark,
 and lichen lingers
over the pulsing rocks.

the trees rekindle their open arms,
where mycelium feeds the fawn.

the green recalls to us everything
we once forgot to return to.
bears and deer keep time
with something deeper than stone,
brighter than ferns.

where the pond lies down
in the arms of the valley,
the hills are home to an ocean —
of bees and birds —
residing deep

Journey of an Herbalist

The leaves and things — crashed into me,
and bore me to the fens —
The medicines and doctors' hems
held me open, then;

Where I could see — the baby deer
and wild mist were growing;
Blending petals taught me how
to counteract a death.

Ginseng spills — across my hands,
ginger through my chest,
and leaves — inlaid — my temples —
the roses hold my hands,

and all the careful, cluttered mess
reveals the floral medicines.
Someone said my power grew;
to listen to the land.

About the Author

Sophia Pinto Thomas is a poet from Boston, Massachusetts. She was born in the early 2000s to a family of artists and social workers. She enjoys experimenting with the possibilities of rhyme, learning from the trials of young adulthood, and observing the miracles of the natural world. Sophia is an eco-poet, world-maker, and eternal student. She posts poetry on her Instagram (@sophiapintothomas), and her free Substack newsletter "Thoughts Across Bostonia".

www.ingramcontent.com/pod-product-compliance
Lightning Source LLC
LaVergne TN
LVRC091353060526
838201LV00041B/413